Wandering Places

A Collection of Poems

Wandering Places

A Collection of Poems

TONYA SNOW-COOK

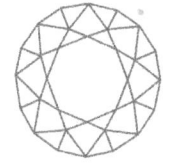

AMETHYST
Publishing

Published by
Amethyst Publishing
info@amethystpublishing.com

Wandering Places © 2017 by Tonya Snow-Cook. All rights reserved. No part of this book may be reproduced in any form or by any means including electronic, mechanical or photocopying or stored in a retrieval system without permission in writing from the publisher except for the use of brief quotations in a book review or scholarly journal.

For more information about the author and upcoming books, visit:
http://www.tonyasnowcook.com

ISBN: 978-0-9715062-2-0

First Printing January 2008
Printed in the United States of America
Fourth Edition

About the Poetry

I think this book is inspired a great deal by the works of the poets and writers, such as Keats, Angelou, Hughes, Wheatley, Poe, Milton, Eliot, Whitman, Marlowe, Dante, who I'd read during both my undergraduate and graduate studies, majoring in English. An English background coupled with my life experiences and a God-given talent to take words and tell a story through verse and prose resulted in the creation of *Wandering Places*. There is a pun on the word "wandering." After reading the book, you'll find that I've written poems not only about physical motion (i.e., walking, drifting, floating, traveling), but also poems about how the mind "wonders" about [or attempts to resolve questions about] or reflects on all sorts of things like love, death, childhood experiences, or life experiences in general. What is life if not a journey: physical, mental, and spiritual?

To reflect my moods of inspiration, this collection of poetry is arranged into five thematic sections: Strolling Thu Wonderland, Black-Eyed Peas & Collard Greens, The Art of Life, Chocolate Shakespeare, and That's Amore. Sometimes I was inspired by my African-American roots and Southern upbringing. Other times I heard Keats or some other poet of the past whispering in my ear. Then, there's the plain ole love for writing, and most times that was enough to inspire a line or two or twenty. For instance, in the section entitled "The Art of Life," I've written poems, some lighthearted, inspired by the age-old tossup between philosophies that art imitates life and life imitates art. The poems in this section are a tribute to the humanities: art, photography, music, drama, writing, etc. This section could easily be re-entitled in the reverse as "The Life of Art," as could this collection of work itself.

Contents

Stroll Thru Wonderland 1
   In Night's Gloom 3
   Sweet Dreams 4
   Seaweed 5
   Muse 6
   Requiem for Roger 7
   Gloster's on the Other Side of Pluto 8
   Displacement 10
   Before There was Sound 12
   Blah 13
   Delicate Rosebud 14
   Summer's Song 15
   High School 16
Black-eyed Peas & Collard Greens 19
   Chicken Soup 21
   A Long Ways Home… 22
   Passing Through 24
   on the bayou 26
   A Blues Tune for Montego 27
   Inner Sanctum 29
The Art of Life 31
   Moonlite Jazz 33
   Chamber Music 34
   The Chase 35
   Dark Room 36
   My Favorite Imagination 37
   So E.T. Wants to Write Poetry 38
   Portrait of a Mocking Bird 39
Chocolate Shakespeare: Ode to Writers Past 41
   12 o'clock 43
   Conversation with the Creator of Quiet, Entry I 44
   Writer's Ode to His Lost Words 46
   If He Dances with the Devil 48
   Fairytale 49
   Educating the Soul 50
That's Amore 51
   As Beauty Speaks 53

Nostalgia 55
You Call That Love?...56
M's Cafe...58
Heartache 59

Tonya Snow-Cook

Stroll Thru Wonderland

"These are the last days, the beginning of the end, it seems—a bleak and inescapable winter ahead. The only thing to look forward to is tomorrow, the hope that something better is on the other side of today."

Wandering Places

Tonya Snow-Cook

In Night's Gloom

Somewhere someone sleeps
On dust cushion and pillow decay.
From a neighboring pine,
A high chord is lilted
But deafened by the grass-root walls,
Walls we have managed to escape.

Somewhere there are those
Who never sleep,
Who kiss the dark with crimson lips,
Who parch the changing skies,
Whose souls hear only chaos
And lay suspended in night's gloom.

Wandering Places

Sweet Dreams

Her face was pale
From lack of sunlight.
Her arms, fallen at her sides.
As the tide undulated,
The figure resembling a rag doll
Motioned with it,
Resting there
On a shallow bed of gray
Like a child tucked away.
And with the sun
Vanishing behind the trees,
Her ocean began to whisper,
"Sweet dreams, my child,
Sweet dreams."

Tonya Snow-Cook

Seaweed

I'd like to walk the beach,
Feel the sand
Run between my toes,
Tickle my feet
With its coolness,
Slide under my heels like silk.

    I want to walk the beach,
    Smell the sand,
    Taste the salt on the air,
    Become as seaweed,
    Washed about by the ocean,
    Having no destination,
    Just going from shore to shore…

Muse

Purple cloaked clouds
Announce the coming of an
Evitable apocalypse.
Obstructing visibility,
Pounding asphalt of yesterday's stench,
Incessantly tapping against
Tinted glass and galvanized cans
And concrete steps and metal doors
That allow strangers in through peepholes
Until it slips through the cracks,
Makes its way up five flights of stairs,
Having realized the out-of-order sign
Taped to the elevator door,
Bothers not to knock, but
Slips under my doorsill
Like magician's smoke and
Hovers over my bed,
Coming to me in tiny whispers
Till it awakens my inner child,
Unsilences my voice,
Becomes the muse.

Tonya Snow-Cook

Requiem for Roger

no more theatrical moments
of hide and seek
no ado by a bob, no scurry to the top
to savor today what is gone tomorrow
when there are two and not one
yet now there is one and not two
with scaly remains dangled
over a porcelain bowl
as the other listens in for those
final notes—PLOP! and FLUSH!

So long my little Carassius Auratus.

Wandering Places

Gloster's on the Other Side of Pluto

We could hear every sound,
every car engine approaching
then gradually faint down
that road of dust and potholes and
make-shift gravel.
First time I traveled that road
I knew I was in another galaxy,
where neighbors only come out
to burn trash in barrels full of bullet holes,
where an echo could still
be heard the next morning.
How could any civilization amass here,
dragging with them, in flocks and droves,
all in which they hold dear,
leaving behind the noises of the city,
traffic jams, screaming sirens,
block party music blaring
from two streets away?
It even smelled different.
Smelled like horse manure and
farm equipment and grass and
when the sun showed absolutely no mercy,
every pungent odor fused together,
creating the essence of this place,
a fusion of smells so lasting I
remember that essence twelve years later
while sitting at my laptop in my office
in my home in the suburb wishing
I had one of those power telescopes
that could bring things on the other

side of Pluto within my reach.

Wandering Places

Displacement

Can't breathe in this place.
Six years of suffocation
And 360 degrees of separation.
Tried to make connections.
Today I remain displaced.
An 8-hour drive was too far
A trip to make for a weekend stay.
No vacation time to take.
Once-a-year visits aren't enough anymore,
So now they come to me in dreams,
Replacing the darkness behind
Closed shutters with friendly colors
And familiar faces.
Wish I could just uproot myself,
Go back to where I belong,
Find my mind some peace
On a cedar porch,
Surrounded by 7 acres of nibbled grass,
A thoroughbred or 2 in the back,
A tire swing that had to come down,
A tether ball string dangling from a metal pole,
A pretend clubhouse with trees for walls
Next to a dried up pond, no, waterless stream,
A tin barn giving shelter to hay bales
And old bikes with rusted chains and tire rot.
I remember when dad brought that yellow
Bicycle made of used parts home.
Years later it became a permanent fixture
In the backyard.

Tonya Snow-Cook

First thing we want to do is get away,
Start something new,
Find a different path to take.
Sometimes what we find is too different,
Too far removed from what we first knew
Or what first shaped who we were to become.
I now know that I had to run away,
Come here, to find my way back.

Before There was Sound

Before there was sound,
There was silence,
Staging its early cinematic presence
With black and white performers whose
Mouths moved, but words fell deaf
On our ears,
Contorted faces showed us fear or
Shock or displeasure or pain.
Doubled-over bodies showed us glee
And pleasure.
From the early picture show,
We've learned to embrace silence,
Learned to listen for meaning in
What is often times shown rather than
Uttered.

Tonya Snow-Cook

Blah

Can vaguely remember the last time
I was dancing on the clouds,
Looking down over your heads
'Cause now I'm low as dust,
Feed off the decay of the land,
Play Cowboys and Indians with the ants.
The sun is so far away
It may as well be the size of a dot.
Misery has me by the throat.
I can never speak again,
Can scarcely remember your name.
You don't even have a face,
Just blah.

Delicate Rosebud

I have dreamt of a day
Not confined by the penalties of time,
An evening in which no one, nothing stops…

From my hammock, I've watched
The flowering of this once delicate rosebud.
Now a mature thing, exchanging between other forms,
Yet still needing the embrace of nature.

A delicate rosebud, this botanical wonder.
Mustn't let wilt the petals under which it's concealed.
If only disconnection brought about no end,
It could be mine to lay beside my lover's pillow.

Tonya Snow-Cook

Summer's Song

A yellow jacket dances around the dandy lion.
A humming bird bounces a chord off fluttering wings.
Summer wheat sways in a neighbor's field
While ambitions settle and nature sings.
Above my head, an azure sky fills
With cloud pictures and shapes and all sorts of things.
Somewhere on a tree branch the locust shrills
As the wind blows across my face.

A few acres away growls the grinding tractor,
Interrupted suddenly by a youngster yelling, "Stop!"
As the other plows in front on his Huffy bicycle,
Leaving me with only the squeal of rubber against blacktop.
I imagine the boys dodging potholes and switching gears
With one fleeing like the robber, the other chasing like a cop
Until a squeaking screen door becomes an echo in their ears,
Reminding them that it's late and time to come in.

Wandering Places

High School

In shuffles a hundred dozen
Feet against the linoleum;
And the Halls of Silence
Erupt with chit and chatter.
Sixteen hours was too long a wait
To see a friend's face,
Or spill the dirt about the neighbor's son's
Run-in with the cops.
Then the clanking of tin doors drowns out
The ringing school bell,
And kids race to home room
Just in time for roll call.
A teacher's scan, a raised hand,
A brief intro then time to go.
Each hour, on the hour, and not a minute late,
Kids rush to periods one thru sixth,
Somewhere in between grabbing a bite to eat
And maybe slipping a note
In a friend's backpack.

High school—that place where
Adolescent optimism is restored
Then lost again after a mother's
Nag or father's insult.
High school—that place where the corridors
Showcase first place trophies
And photos of principals and teachers
And staff members long gone.
High school—that place where the
Beginning ends and the end begins.

High school.

Wandering Places

Tonya Snow-Cook

Black-eyed Peas & Collard Greens

"In her novel *The Color Purple*, Alice Walker alludes that God put the color purple on earth in hopes that we might notice it. If so, perhaps a tree was put in plain sight for the same purpose, that we might notice the color green."

Wandering Places

Tonya Snow-Cook

Chicken Soup

I can almost taste
But it's too hot.
I'll burn my tongue,
So I'll let it cool.
Juicy chunks that sink
To the bottom and drown.
The smell, luring aroma,
Drifting along the hall
Through the door
Up into my nostrils.
I close my eyes
And inhale slowly
As if it were my last chance
At something wonderful
While it calls,
"Come, come, come devour."
What temptation!
I must…but I can't.
I may get burned.
I'm too weak,
Too weak to resist.
At least, I'll take
My defeat with content.
Oooooh!
The agony.

Wandering Places

A Long Ways Home...

As I stare out the winda,
Down onto the passin' trees,
I stretch my feeble eyes
Far across those golden pastures
Of Autumn's song
And I see an ol' raggedy barn
With a rusty tin roof.
And I just smile
'Cause it reminds me
Of my childhood.

I rememba the...
The summa heat that drove us
Out of the house into the streets
And the sound the rope made against
The pavement
And ol' white folk passin' by
In them fancy box-wheels
And mama callin', "Come in child,
Time fa suppa."

Now aged with history,
I sit here and watch this ol' world
Pass me by.
My mind make me strong,
But these ol' bones of mine
Are gon' suffa
Till my time come.
In the meantime,
I'm just gon' ride this here train

Tonya Snow-Cook

'Cause I'm a long ways home.

Wandering Places

Passing Through

I knew glory once.
It was simply passing through
Like a barge on the great Mississippi
Or a light breeze at noon.
The days were longer then
And the sun delivered a smile
Just about everyday.
Hearing that ice cream truck
A block away was always a blessing.
But like the barge and the breeze,
Glory was just passing through.

I knew sadness once.
I watched it mosey up
As I sat outside a bus depot,
Reading the paper.
"Our Country was in shambles," it read.
No one seemed to mind.
Birds lined the telephone cable
To sing their daily anthem.
Like always, George, the milkman,
Slipped Miss Dotson an extra bottle,
Hoping she'd say "yes."
And like clockwork, she'd wait
Till he left, come to the door,
Look down at her porch and smile.
I reckon like the barge and the breeze
And those busy afternoons
When life bounced about town
Until it was time for calm to settle,

Tonya Snow-Cook

Sadness was just passing through, too.

on the bayou

i'd heard it so many times…it's what
everybody says, what most people think
so I went there thinking I'd catch a glimpse
of voodoo's only child while
crypt keepers watched their coffins
float down the murky gulf and fanged demons
lived on ecstasy stealing their poisons
from warm-blooded corpses
but what I found was
swamps and lakes and mossy trees
southern jazz, humming bees
gumbo spice and cajun rice
buzzing chatter of creo tongues
white picket fences around plantation homes
mardi gras floats and river boats
greetings with a smile, hand shakes good-bye
two toppings of ice-cream over warm apple pie
ringing church bells, fireworks on christmas eve
leaves changing hues in autumn
changing again in spring
so the next time you run into somebody
who's talking that crazy talk about woodoo
point them to me—let me tell 'em
what's really on the bayou

Tonya Snow-Cook

A Blues Tune for Montego

What saddened me most was knowing that,
While this place is a tourist mecca,
Grandmothers with amputated limbs cane
Their daughters' children when they don't
Approach the tourist van stopped at a traffic
Light fast enough to panhandle or peddle
Sticks of gum for a dollar.
I hardly understand why the export of sugar cane
And bananas has had so little effect on commerce
Or residential and commercial development;
And, as we passed through the countryside in a
Charter bus, it buzzing with chatter, mostly of
Fellow tourists discussing their day-to-day itinerary
Of swimming, paddle boating, snorkeling, and the like,
It seemed that every local was on an extended holiday,
Because, as I later learned, there were very, very few jobs,
Not even those we from the states would hardly
Consider glamorous.
I saw only make-shift fruit stands next to lean-tos,
And the highlight was stopping at a sort of flea market
Where sold were hundreds of wooden carvings,
Wooden elephants and wooden frogs, wooden canes
With eagle heads, woven baskets and wooden bead
Necklaces, and incense of course.
If you couldn't find what you were looking for
In one booth, then you were sure to find it
In the booth next to or across from it.
How eager they were for our business,
How willing they were to knock off a dollar
Or two, realizing how easy it would be to

Wandering Places

Lose any money to the man or woman two
Booths down.
"At least, the resort is nice," offered someone.
"'At least, the resort is nice.'"
WOW, have we become so numb to things like
This?

Tonya Snow-Cook

Inner Sanctum

Whenever I need an escape,
I reach deep inside me, down in my spirit,
Where clanging tambourines and choral voices
Drown out credit card monsters and traffic jams
And grocery lines that wrap around the building.
Jesus loves me this I know, because the Bible tells
Me so and because...
He gives me words to write when I am here.
He gives me thoughts to think when I am here.
Why does my caged bird sing? I sing because
Jesus gave me a song. He dropped a melody in my soul
And now my soul keeps dancing.
He placed the lyrics in my heart and my hands
Keep clapping.
I am the congregation, swinging and swaying,
Stumping and shouting inside Holy walls with
Stained-glass windows—these Holy walls.
These Holy walls are inside me, down in my spirit,
Down in my spirit, where clanging tambourines and
Choral voices drown out car payments and tuition fees and
Labor unions and credit card monsters and traffic jams
And grocery lines that wrap around the building.

Wandering Places

Tonya Snow-Cook
The Art of Life

"Somehow art is a way for us to pattern ourselves after God when He created this place."

Wandering Places

Moonlite Jazz

Billions of starlites
Under a half moon
Caress the soft tenders
Of an old gent's only passion.
He hides these burnings
During the day
So his face remains unseen, unknown.
At midnight, his fingers engage
In countless play before a dance
Of bright eyes gleaming desire.
It is the sacred intimacy between nature
And his depths, fears, longings...
His sea of chaos
Molding into existence,
His one sincerity
Making ripples in the wind,
For above the heavens
Where angels lay,
His one true LOVE
For a child who never dies.

Wandering Places

Chamber Music

Four young men dressed in black
Tapped on my chamber door.
"What do you want?" I asked of them.
To play for you till four.
"Till four, you say?"
Till four, we say.
Have you no ears to hear?
"I do, young men. How dare you ask?
And yes, please do come in."

Each a seat sat he quite still
And tuned his instrument fine.
"Till four, you say?"
Till four, we say.
"For this, I must have wine."
The cello laughed.
The flute sang.
The oboe danced with the violin.
When the hour drew, chamber music ceased
And quiet ruled once again.

Tonya Snow-Cook

The Chase

I lay peacefully in my bed.
On downy pillow, I rest my head.
A beautiful concerto, "Symphony Fantastique"
Serenades my spirit as it sleeps.

In comes the lowly cadenza of a French horn
Dancing in syncopation with the other horns.
When suddenly the tympani takes a WACK,
Turning what once was calm into a mad dash.

Men of distinct valor with fine instruments in chase
With the French horn dashing frantically to win the race
Through thicket and branches, over hills, through trees.
"Faster, Faster!" it exclaims. "Let's win this, please!"

Enough! Enough! Fate makes its blow.
The chase has ended and away they go.
To chambers each instrument soon retires
Until the symphonic muse next inspires.

Dark Room

Dimensions not seen at first
Fading slowly into real
What a rush!
Mysterious faces
Zoomed in by a naked eye
Then trapped in a tiny black box
He sees everything as something
To be photographed,
An art to share with the world,
Showing the depths
Of mankind and nature,
Creating a way
That time may delay forever
In which moments become not just memories,
But framed realities.

Tonya Snow-Cook

My Favorite Imagination

The curtains are drawn.
The audience is silenced.
The stage lights up
On Love and Hate engaged
In heightened melodrama,
Hate, heartless baron, storms
Into a bitter outrage, cursing life,
Cursing liberty, cursing happiness,
For it knows no other
Form of expression,
Feels no light, wants only darkness,
Was the foster child of Anger and Contempt,
Long estranged was the mother
Who first nursed it,
Who first shaped its thoughts,
Whose other offspring, Love,
Was never orphaned.
Now center stage, Hate confronts his brother,
Wanting nothing more than
To strike Love down with
His sword of Envy and drain life,
But Love returns only kindness.
For every blow attempted,
Kindness is returned,
Sending Hate into an even maddened state
And the audience into a deafening roar
Till, finally, the succession of unsuccesses,
Sends Hate exiting left,
Leaving only the invincible Love.

Wandering Places

So E.T. Wants to Write Poetry

I read this poem just to pass the day,
But the bloody thing was in pretty bad shape.
Who taught this idiot such unimaginable words,
Words nobody I knew had ever heard.
Oh, I read it again and again until I figured it out—
This babbling idiot was an alien, no doubt.
Must have come from another planet during another bloody time,
From some off-the-wall galaxy where they don't teach rhyme.
So I tossed it aside because enough was enough!
Went and found me a feathered pen to write my own darn stuff.

Tonya Snow-Cook

Portrait of a Mocking Bird

I sat and watched a mocking bird
Quench its thirst from a mere.
Then it stretched its gray neck a bit,
As if to aid digestion, or
Perhaps it was doing something else.
Could it have been that I was witnessing
A new form of communication, which had
Evolved that day between man and bird?
Might this magnificent creature been aware
That it was now the subject of a local artist,
Imitating with water colors and acrylics
As this mocking bird had often done through song?
To think that it had struck that pose so long
That its parts grew stiff—my goodness!
Could it have been that its back ached from bending
And its stick-like stems stung from standing?
Nevertheless, it stood, a model bird,
Allowing the painter to create on canvas
A portrait that grew more real with each
Brilliant stroke of detail.

Wandering Places

Tonya Snow-Cook

Chocolate Shakespeare: Ode to Writers Past

"I'm inspired most by people who go out and do the things I never believed I could do."

Wandering Places

12 o'clock

Peace be still, my little ones,
Lay now your heads
Upon the prairies of midnight,
Let morning dew settle,
Feeble minds rest,
And hearts dance their dance.

And Poe, My dear friend, Poe,
Do you dream of darling Lenore?
For in the hour of content
Sweat dreams are dreamt
And long-lost flames rekindled.

When that hour is come, day is restored
And Fate claims yet another.
Survivors greet the morning,
Some live out routines,
Others search for new meaning,
Realizing time is forever constant.

Wandering Places

Conversation with the Creator of Quiet, Entry I

Atlas, I've let myself be enslaved
Despite that intense ringing in my head
Of them singing their Savior into existence,
"Come release these shackles from me!"
And I, too, summons my own savior through song…
Come, creator of the quiet world,
Exile me from this natural wasteland,

This landfill of political pollution
And scientific dada and anarchy
And social corruption and propaganda
And games and charades and circus acts.

Many days I've gone inside myself
To seek the pleasures of my mind.
For in the clenches of maddening chaos,
When hatred and love war the plane,
When life and liberty scarcely exist,
When time runs its *Swiftest* pace,
I thirst for quiet.
Not the quiet of idleness
That spoils the innocent soul
Nor the quiet of stillness
That anchors the Dead.
Mustn't let my spirit feed off chaotic vines,
Mustn't parent ruined grapes,
Mustn't imbibe the sweet taste of pleasure wines
That intoxicate the mental self.

Oh, Cosmos, dear friend, I've found my truth

Tonya Snow-Cook

As you have found yours—

The quiet of meaning is the meaning of quiet.

And I do submit

As you have yielded to your "true self."
Let it haunt me, tease me, inspire the rhyme,
Awaken the genius within.

Wandering Places

Writer's Ode to His Lost Words

      1
Has it not been far, far too long awhile
   Since I've felt the gentleness of your caress
Or heard your whisper through the rustle of a leaf pile?
   For without you, existence is meaningless.
Surely you've missed those moments we exchanged,
    For new meaning have I given neglect,
     But should there be so high a price for abandonment
Now that we've been seven years estranged,
    And will no sorrow passing these lips ever perfect
       An apology worthy to pacify your discontent?

      2
But curse no longer this desperate soul,
   Release from my mind these wretched chains,
Light under me the fire with which to compose
   Verse celebrating Milton's gains,
Or Keat's attempt to freeze time and space
   On a Grecian urn, out of which pours no ash,
    Or the irony that man and myth are in part the same,
Yet neither at history's end shall leave a trace,
   Not even I will have a place in which to dash,
     It's only now that I remain in each page I etch my name.

     3
For seven long years, I'd often dream
   That I was a master of imagery,
And most prolific in rhyme and scheme,
   And followed all rules of poetry;
But reality has left me only to assume

Tonya Snow-Cook

Some day you'll return to the likes of me,
    Who sometimes rejects convention for style,
And sometimes excavates from Eliot's tomb
    An ode or two of revelry,
        And treats each word as if a child.

Wandering Places

If He Dances with the Devil

There is a single task,
Which shall gain you the formula
To quiet your lady's rave.
At the dry of your signet,
You shall know all things.
Yes, all things you shall know.
Dear old, faithful Faustus[1],
I know the cunnings of curiosity,
This lady of lure,
Who rants of what secrets lie
Beyond the who, what, why, or how.
She let's not a single day's passing
Without drifting into your conscience.

Careful, my friend,
She is a titled temptress,
Winning her every round.
It is not enough for her to have
Your conscious thoughts;
She must also have your sleep.
She jabs at your dreams,
Requiring your immediate awake
Until you suffer a deprivation
Beyond speech.
So sign, sign, dear friend, just sign,
And I will end the madness;
We shall have the last dance.

1. Christopher Marlow's Dr. Faustus, who sells his soul to the devil for infinite knowledge.

Tonya Snow-Cook

Fairytale

She gazed heavily upon her lover's painting,
Tracing with her eyes his every line,
Curve, and curl as if she'd seen an apparition
Of dear departed Beowulf.
Myriads of tears trickled her face while she
Reminisced on foregoing enchantment.
He, whom she so adored, whom she loved
In great measure, confessed his love for another.
Had not her beauty entitled her to the most elite?
Yet, she had been replaced by someone of lesser affair.
And there was nothing left to do, but give into
The madness, so into the madness she did give,
Spilling the blood of vines down her throat until
She collapsed and lay drunk.

Wandering Places

Educating the Soul

two years
I staggered in limbo.
my time was far-spent
in survey of direction,
but there was no path certain to me then.
on occasion,
sweet slumber nursed my exhaustion
and dreams were an escape
from my uncertain reality.
I summoned Patience to aid,
but her virtue proved finer suited for the pauper,
whose daily discontent and destitution
was displayed on a beggar's sign.
my lack of faith compromised her stay
but Fate sent her away.
never was my task more despised
and Misery more the companion,
her incessant chatter, urging—
urging me to seek refuge
among the faceless masses of Purgatory,
whose vile deeds had tainted the family name
and angered the Heavens.

in deed, there is a price
for searching within these walls
what might easily be found in one's backyard.

in memory of the struggle with grad school

Tonya Snow-Cook

That's Amore

"Sometimes love is pain; other times love is the cure."

Wandering Places

Tonya Snow-Cook

As Beauty Speaks

Before there was you,
I was afraid of the hour and of the hour's end,
Afraid of the dust, afraid of the wind,
Afraid of the trees, afraid of the ocean,
Afraid of the sky, afraid of the evening,
Afraid of the sunset and of the sun's rising.
Then beauty revealed to me
That which it whispered to the poet
And to the poet's lover and to the lover's keeper.
No longer do I toil with fear.
No longer do I reject my predecessors.
T'is written, "Better to have loved and lost…"
Atlas, I know love.
Perhaps I haven't the most profound words to describe you.
Somehow I've misplaced my genius,
But this I know:
Whenever my eyes are filled with your image,
My heart abandons its restless state.

I remember our first encounter, how beauty spoke to me.
The heat in that café was torrid, the windows opened to chaos.
I sat at breakfast, sipping my tea, watching the fading images
When you rustled in from the busy streets and scourging sun.
Your body carried that familiar smell of outside
And a warm feeling came over me.
I was reminded of a long-forgotten childhood,
Playing in the swaying wheat field,
Stealing melons from the neighbor's patch.
Our eyes met and I knew.

Wandering Places

Before there was you, there was another.
Someone whose love was a wretched thing.
Oh, how easily the heart is blinded
And the mind is fooled.
Yes, that encounter left me empty, so empty
I shut out the trees and saw only a gray sky,
I saw no beauty in the sunset, no promise in the sun's rising.
I longed for the evening, and even more for evening's end.
Then self-pity grew into anger and anger into fear.
I was afraid to trust and afraid to want,
Afraid to feel and afraid to not,
Afraid to live and afraid to die,
Afraid to shutdown and afraid to cry.
Afraid of the hour and of the hour's end,
Afraid of the dust, afraid of the wind,
Afraid of the trees, afraid of the ocean,
Afraid of the sky, afraid of the evening,
Afraid of the sunset and of the sun's rising.
Afraid of nothing and afraid of everything.

Then I saw you and beauty spoke to me.

Tonya Snow-Cook

Nostalgia

N O S T A L G I A,
That's what I feel whenever I utter your name
Or remember your face,
Or how you'd dance your jig to goof around.
When I think of home, I think of you
And that boyish look you'd have when
You wanted to be playful,
Or the tap on my shoulder you'd give
With the secret message hidden in it,
But what you tried to say, I already knew.
Your patterns rarely changed;
Your routine stayed nearly the same,
But that's what I'd grown to appreciate
Most about you, that's what made me feel
Safe when you were around.
And, someday, when the little one's old
Enough to understand, I'll share with her what
Made her father such a wonderful man.

Wandering Places

You Call That Love?

We uttered those vows ten years ago.
You were young. We both were.
I was in love with love.
You were…well, you always said
That you were in love with me.
How beautiful you were.
How you were my superman.
You were going to save me from my world,
Lift me up right out of my miserable life
And fly me straight to the moon or Mars
Or Saturn or somewhere, anywhere, but there.
You did. You wore the goofy glasses by day
And strapped on the boots and
Crimson cape by night.
My Clark Kent, you were,
But you were more than that.
You were afternoon walks in Paris.
A streetcar ride in San Francisco.
A cool glass of lemonade on a veranda in the country.
A day at the beach sun bathing.
The echo of giggling kids miles away.
The rainbow after the rain.
The sound of music in the seasons.
That favorite bite to eat.
That black and white romance
That wrenches every tear from my being.
A rose left on a lover's pillow.
That first dance, that first kiss.
The way the sun rises from behind the mountains.
The coolness of a light breeze.

Tonya Snow-Cook

The smell of lilac in the air.
That favorite baseball team winning.
You were my everything.
A long stroll thru wonderland.
Black-eyed peas and collard greens.
The art of life. The life of art.
My chocolate Shakespeare.
My first and only amore.
I couldn't express that enough.
And you were not supposed to turn to me one day
And say good-bye. You call that Love?

Wandering Places

M's Cafe

Single-level brownstone,
Flickering neon,
A shortage somewhere in the main line,
"That gives it character," someone offers.
Gargantuan glass entry way for the
Larger-than-life night owls;
Big tippers, big spenders running up tabs
Into the next year, entitled to their own table,
Their names carved into the back of chairs;
Regulars, they have come to be known,
Receiving the special V.I.P. phone call
When some new act is in town.
It's no exotico, but the music's good.
Dimly lit booths are the perfect ambiance
For a sneaking glance or a lover's dance.
Isn't that what it's all about--the romance?
Yeah, that's exactly what it's all about

—the romance…

Tonya Snow-Cook

Heartache

Careful not to numb when
Heartache has staked its claim.
Never a thousand and one tears shed,
Nor in a cold bed with stranger lay.
Let heartache mend with the spooling of time,
Creep for only its season
Until your lowly soul hears music again.

Wandering Places

www.ingramcontent.com/pod-product-compliance
Lightning Source LLC
Chambersburg PA
CBHW031423040426
42444CB00005B/686